AIDS

Designed and produced by
Aladdin Books Ltd
70 Old Compton Street
London W1

First published in the
United States in 1987 by
Gloucester Press
387 Park Avenue South
New York, NY 10016

Library of Congress Catalog
Card Number 87-80449

ISBN 0-531-17054-3

The author, Nigel Hawkes, is diplomatic correspondent of The Observer
newspaper, London.

The consultant, Anthony J. Pinching, BM BCh MA DPhil FRCP, is
Clinical Immunologist, St Mary's Hospital Medical School, London.

The back cover photograph shows how the AIDS virus appears under
an electron microscope.

Contents

AIDS kills	4
The time bomb	6
A new disease	8
The AIDS virus	10
How AIDS spreads	12
AIDS in Africa	14
AIDS: the symptoms	17
Testing for AIDS	18
Avoiding AIDS	21
Preventing AIDS	22
Can AIDS be treated?	24
Living with AIDS	26
The unknown future?	28
Hard facts	30
Index	32

AIDS

NIGEL HAWKES

Illustrated by
Ron Hayward Associates

Gloucester Press
New York : London : Toronto : Sydney

AIDS kills

Since 1981 a new terrifying disease has been threatening the world. It is called AIDS – Acquired Immune Deficiency Syndrome – and it has no cure. Everybody who develops AIDS will die – though not immediately. Dying of AIDS is a long and often lonely battle against a variety of unpleasant symptoms.

Anyone can catch AIDS – man, woman and child. It is a contagious disease – passed on from person to person – through sexual contact or in the blood. Most countries consider AIDS to be the major health crisis of this century. In the United States, 16,000 people have already died. By 1991, nearly 100,000 will have been stricken and 10 million will be carrying the virus. In Africa, where AIDS is far more widespread, no one knows exactly how many thousands of people have lost their lives.

Fortunately, by knowing how the AIDS virus infection is spread, it can be avoided by quite simple precautions. This book will tell you about AIDS: how it is caught, how it kills, and how you can protect yourself from it.

▷ Ken Ramsaur, an American AIDS victim, appealed on television for more efforts to find a cure for the disease that was killing him. Ramsaur was one of the early victims of AIDS; he died in July 1983 soon after making his appeal.

AIDS worldwide

Worldwide, AIDS has been detected in virtually every country which has a health system sophisticated enough to detect it. It is becoming a worldwide epidemic. Over the next ten to 20 years it will cause millions of deaths.

The **United States** is the worst affected country outside Africa, with 32,000 AIDS cases, of whom over 16,000 have already died. Within five years 1,000 people a week will be dying of AIDS. At the moment, 220 people die each week.

The **United Kingdom** has many fewer AIDS patients: no more than 600 people have so far contracted AIDS. Most of the cases – 430 out of the 600 – are in London. In 1987, two people will die of AIDS each day.

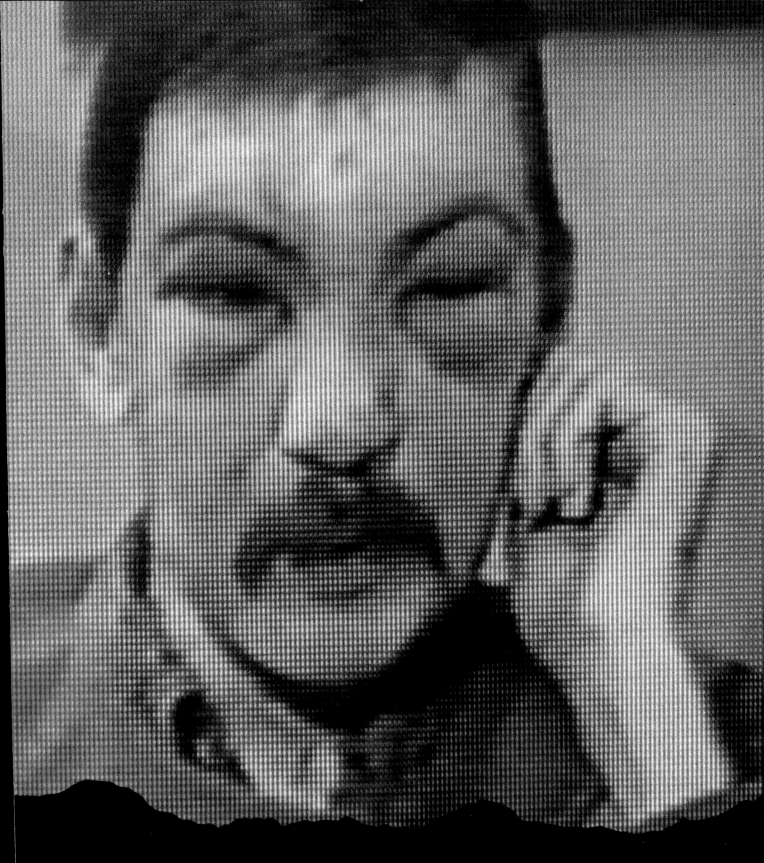

France has so far recorded a total of 1,050 AIDS patients, of whom 466 have died. About 15 new cases appear each week. The great majority – 85 per cent – are men, but the proportion of women with AIDS is rising.

Central Africa almost certainly has more AIDS cases than the rest of the world put together. Some experts believe that at least one million Africans will die of AIDS in the next ten years. The ratio of men to women is 11 to ten.

Brazil is the worst affected country in Latin America, with 841 known cases of AIDS and 420 deaths. The number of cases is expected to rise to 8,000 in the next few years. Other Latin American countries have no figures.

All figures are from 1986

The time bomb

As of 1987 32,000 AIDS cases have been reported in the United States. The US government estimates 50,000 to 125,000 people show signs of HIV infection and 1.5 million may carry the virus but so far show no symptoms of the disease.

Why does AIDS spread so rapidly? AIDS is caused by a virus – a tiny organism which attacks the body's defense system. If the defense system is destroyed by the virus, then the body can no longer fight off illness and infection. However, one of the strange things about this virus is that it can also live in the body for years *without* causing harm. Therefore, many people who carry the AIDS virus look and feel completely fit – they show no symptoms of the illness. In fact, AIDS is usually spread by people free of symptoms. This means that no one knows exactly how many people carry the virus. Nor does anyone know for certain how many of these "carriers" will eventually develop AIDS itself – usually called "full-blown AIDS." AIDS is a time bomb: for as long as unsuspecting and healthy people do not take precautions, the virus will continue to spread.

▷ After AIDS had been identified in the United States, the number of recognized cases grew very rapidly, doubling in less than a year. Because as many as 1½ million Americans carry the AIDS virus, it is certain that the number of AIDS sufferers will go on increasing. The graph shows the number of *new* cases reported each year. The slower rate of rise in 1986 should not obscure the fact that the numbers of cases are still rising fast.

1986: under 9,000 (projected figures)

1985: 9,221

1984: 5,503

1983: 2,758

1982: 998

1981: 260

1980: 76

pre-1980: 0

The AIDS virus is transmitted in three ways. First by intimate sexual contact (heterosexual or homosexual), second when the blood of someone who has the virus gets into the blood of another person, and third when it passes from the blood of an infected woman to an unborn child she is carrying.

Before it was understood that the virus is transmitted through the blood, hemophiliacs – people who need special blood products such as Factor VIII to help their blood clot – were given contaminated blood. Many have since died.

△ Patrick Burke is a hemophiliac who was infected with the AIDS virus through a blood product. At the time, nobody was aware of AIDS, or knew it could be transmitted in blood. He passed the virus on to his wife. When she became pregnant she gave the virus to her unborn son. The boy died in 1985. Only the Burkes' daughter, born before the disease struck, is free of AIDS.

A new disease

The first cases of AIDS were identified in the United States in 1981. Doctors at the Centers for Disease Control in Atlanta, Georgia, detected a common thread linking a handful of reports sent to them from New York and Los Angeles. They involved young homosexual men suffering from unusual infections like pneumocystis pneumonia or a rare tumor called Kaposi's sarcoma.

Then in the fall of 1981 the first cases involving drug addicts who injected drugs using shared needles were reported from New York, and in January 1982 a hemophiliac from Miami developed the same symptoms. More cases were being seen all the time and seemed to be caused by some type of virus. What was it? Something new or a new version of something old?

Two groups of scientists went in search of the AIDS virus at the same time. Both teams were trying to piece together the AIDS jigsaw with great urgency.

The French team led by Dr. Luc Montagnier (left) and the American team led by Dr. Robert Gallo (right) raced to identify the virus. Both teams published their claims in the same issue of *Science* magazine in May 1983. But neither claim was conclusive. When Gallo eventually managed to grow enough of the virus in November 1983, what he found surprised him.

Dr. Robert Gallo, a scientist at the National Cancer Institute near Washington DC, suspected that a virus called Human T-cell Leukemia Virus-I (HTLV-I) or something close to it might be responsible. At about the same time a French group from the Pasteur Institute in Paris, led by Dr. Luc Montagnier, found a new virus, which they called lymphadenopathy-associated virus (LAV).

Gallo's group discovered how to "grow" the virus from AIDS patients and was therefore able to find out a lot more about it. They found it was not HTLV-I, but what seemed a similar virus. They called it HTLV-III though it soon turned out to be virtually identical to LAV. Recently the virus has been renamed HIV (Human Immunodeficiency Virus), and this name is used internationally.

The virus he had managed to grow was not the same as the one he had claimed to be the cause of AIDS six months earlier. It turned out to be a variant of the virus the French had discovered. The two are shown in the pictures held by Montagnier — at the top is the American HTLV-III virus, at the bottom the French LAV virus. Since then a great deal has been done by both teams and by others including mapping the complete genetic code of the virus. The team went on to discover how the HIV virus takes over the DNA of the host cell, the cell it enters.

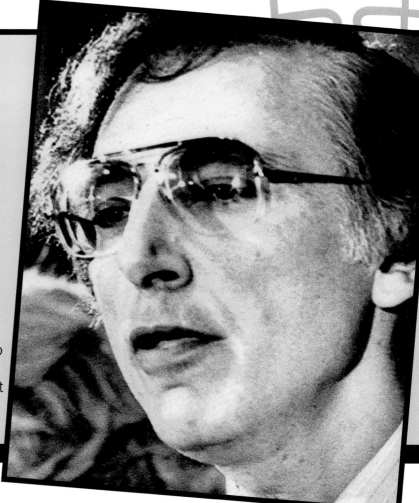

The AIDS virus

Once the HIV virus had been isolated, scientists could concentrate on finding out exactly how it worked. Like all other viruses it works by invading cells and taking them over. Many common diseases – including mumps, chicken pox, measles, colds and flu – are caused by viruses.

However, different viruses attack different kinds of cells. The HIV virus, which causes AIDS, attacks particular cells of the "immune system" – the body's defense system against disease. Once in contact with a virus, special cells of the immune system produce "antibodies" against the virus but they cannot eliminate it. Taken over and crippled by the HIV virus, the immune system can no longer function properly – it becomes "deficient." In fact, special cells of the immune system – the T cells – actually start to produce more of the HIV virus. Without the protection of the immune system, the body is vulnerable to many other infections which seize the opportunity to invade. These are called "opportunistic" infections. It is these infections, not HIV, which cause the symptoms of AIDS.

The AIDS virus invades T cells. Inside the cell the virus undergoes a series of changes. Through the operation of a complex enzyme (reverse transcriptase), the virus copies its RNA to produce DNA, which eventually inserts itself into the DNA of the T cell. Once taken over, the cell then manufactures new virus particles.

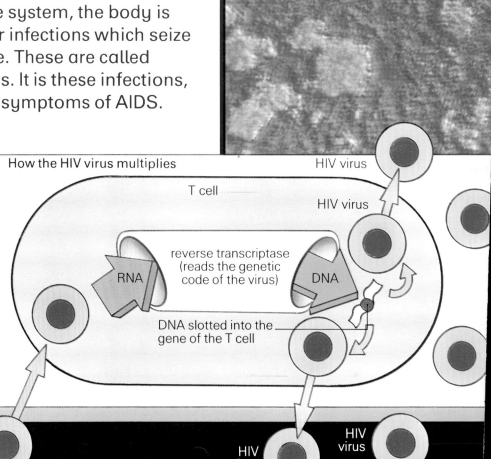

How the HIV virus multiplies

HIV virus

T cell

HIV virus

reverse transcriptase (reads the genetic code of the virus)

RNA

DNA

DNA slotted into the gene of the T cell

HIV virus

HIV virus

HIV virus

HIV virus

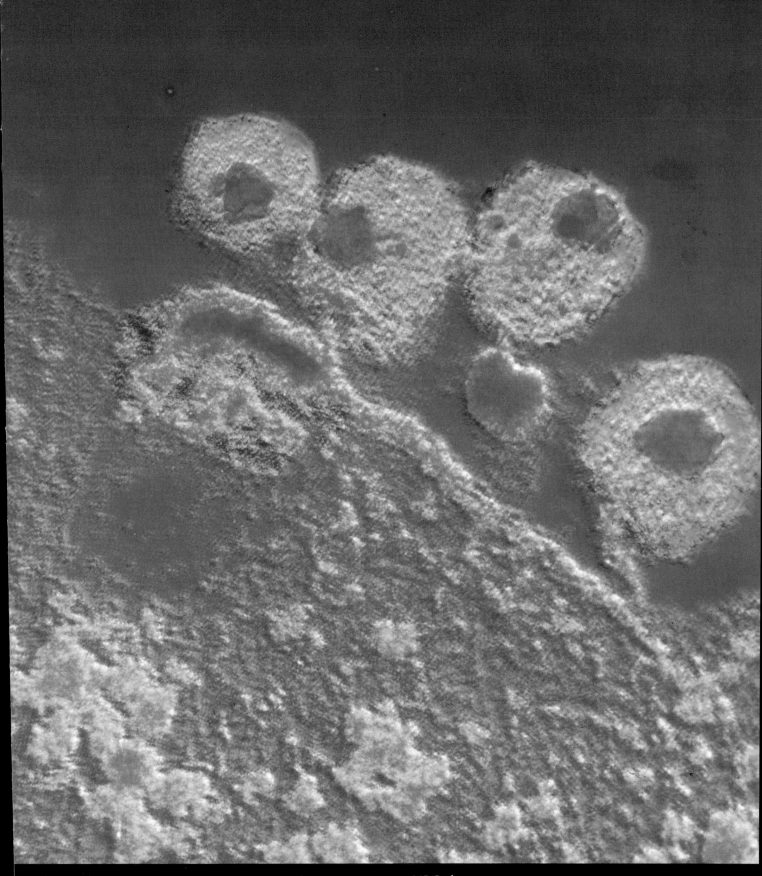

△ Magnified under an electron microscope — new AIDS virus particles form as "buds" on the surface of the T cells

How AIDS can be caught

● Sexual transmission is by far the most likely way to catch AIDS. Although AIDS is more widespread among homosexuals in the West, the virus can attack anyone. Once a man harbors the virus, he can pass it on to a woman in vaginal intercourse. A woman who carries the virus can pass it on to another man.

● The second biggest group of people infected with the AIDS virus in the United States are drug addicts who use hypodermic needles to inject heroin or other drugs. Sharing needles and syringes is a way of transferring small traces of blood from person to person.

● AIDS can be caught from contaminated blood. The third largest group is hemophiliacs, about 1% of cases.

● Ordinary blood transfusions can also transmit AIDS, if the blood is contaminated. This risk and the risk of contaminated Factor VIII have been eliminated, at least in the developed countries, by the screening of blood donors and by heat-treating blood.

● The most tragic group of all are unborn babies who catch the disease from their mothers. 245 such cases have been found in the United States and there are many hundreds in Africa.

12

How AIDS spreads

AIDS can affect anyone: in Africa it is found in men and women in equal numbers. However, in Europe and North America, the disease is more widespread in certain groups. These are homosexuals or male bisexuals (who make up 66 per cent of all cases in the United States), drug addicts (17%) and hemophiliacs who have been treated with blood products contaminated by the virus.

Most of those suffering from the disease have gotten AIDS from intimate sexual contact. The evidence suggests that anal intercourse between homosexual men is the most common way to catch the disease. Although homosexuals with the greatest number of partners face the highest risk, AIDS is not a homosexual disease. Anyone who has sex with an infected person is at risk. *And the more partners, male or female, the bigger the risk of coming in contact with someone who carries the virus.*

Drug addicts who share needles and syringes and thus transfer small amounts of blood are also at great risk of contracting AIDS. Hemophiliacs and those given blood transfusions no longer face such risks, because blood is now screened for the virus before use, and blood products are heat-treated to destroy it. There is no risk involved in donating blood.

● AIDS is not very easy to catch. Unlike other viruses, such as those causing the common cold or flu, it cannot be carried in the air, picked up from food, or caught from any other normal social contact. It cannot be caught from shared cups or silverware.

● There is no reason why a child carrying the AIDS virus should not continue to attend a normal school, or an adult continue to work. Some parents have reacted hysterically, thinking that their children could catch the disease from a hemophiliac child at school.

● Sharing a toilet, which often worries people, presents no infection hazard. Nor does shaking hands, cuddling or even kissing, though doctors recommend that those carrying the virus should not engage in deep kissing with the tongue. This is because the virus has been detected in saliva, though there is no evidence it has ever been transmitted in this way.

● Doctors and nurses do not take special risks, as long as they take precautions. Any blood from a carrier – from a cut, say – should be cleaned up immediately. Washing the hands under hot running water with ordinary soap will get rid of the virus. Detergents and heat kill the virus.

◁ Drug addicts who share needles run a high risk of infection. In Holland, addicts who return a used needle are issued with a new, clean one. There is some evidence that this is slowing the spread of the virus, which affects one in 20 of Amsterdam's addicts. But critics of the "free needle" policy claim that it might encourage drug-taking and cannot be justified.

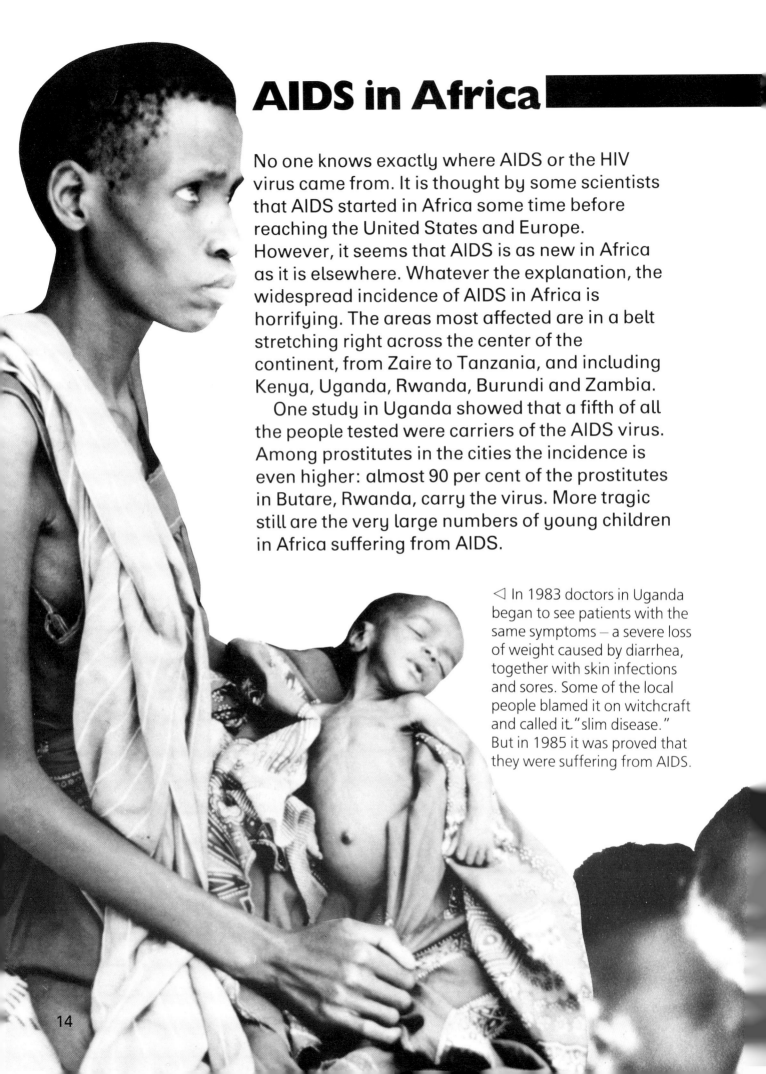

AIDS in Africa

No one knows exactly where AIDS or the HIV virus came from. It is thought by some scientists that AIDS started in Africa some time before reaching the United States and Europe. However, it seems that AIDS is as new in Africa as it is elsewhere. Whatever the explanation, the widespread incidence of AIDS in Africa is horrifying. The areas most affected are in a belt stretching right across the center of the continent, from Zaire to Tanzania, and including Kenya, Uganda, Rwanda, Burundi and Zambia.

One study in Uganda showed that a fifth of all the people tested were carriers of the AIDS virus. Among prostitutes in the cities the incidence is even higher: almost 90 per cent of the prostitutes in Butare, Rwanda, carry the virus. More tragic still are the very large numbers of young children in Africa suffering from AIDS.

◁ In 1983 doctors in Uganda began to see patients with the same symptoms – a severe loss of weight caused by diarrhea, together with skin infections and sores. Some of the local people blamed it on witchcraft and called it "slim disease." But in 1985 it was proved that they were suffering from AIDS.

14

Because the AIDS virus is common among women of child-bearing age, many African children become infected before birth.

Almost all those children affected with AIDS are under five years old, partly because the rapid spread of AIDS is recent, partly because few children infected with the virus survive to their fifth birthday.

The main group of sufferers are young men and women, which confirms that in Africa, as in Europe, AIDS is transmitted sexually. However, in Africa it has spread almost entirely through heterosexual contact.

With fewer resources and inadequate health care, many Africans have also contracted AIDS through contaminated blood. Countries too poor to screen their blood products are still using contaminated blood in transfusions.

African statistics are far less complete than those for Europe and the United States. Poverty, the lack of a comprehensive health system and the reluctance of some governments to admit the scale of the problem have all hindered the gathering of accurate information. But so far the virus has been found in at least 23 African countries.

Kenya is one of the few African countries to have gathered statistics. It has a population of 20 million, and up to four per cent carry the virus. In Uganda up to ten per cent of the sexually active population carry the virus.

African countries urgently need money both to establish how widespread AIDS is and to provide better treatment for sufferers. Without help, they have little chance of slowing the spread.

▽ Many of the babies now being born in Africa are infected with the AIDS virus from their mothers. In some cities, ten per cent of pregnant women attending clinics carry the virus; half their babies will have it too. In Zambia, doctors fear that thousands of AIDS babies will be born in 1987.

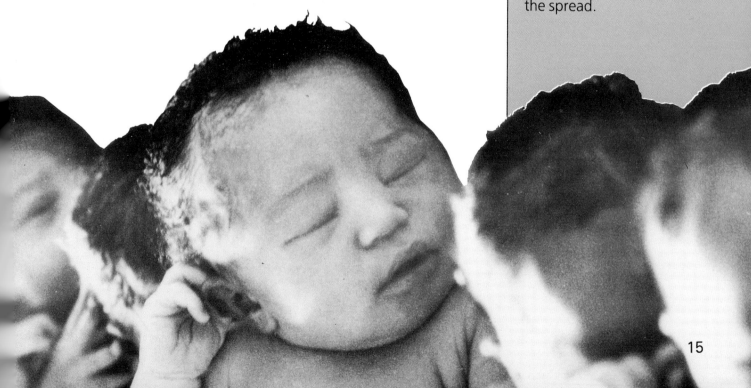

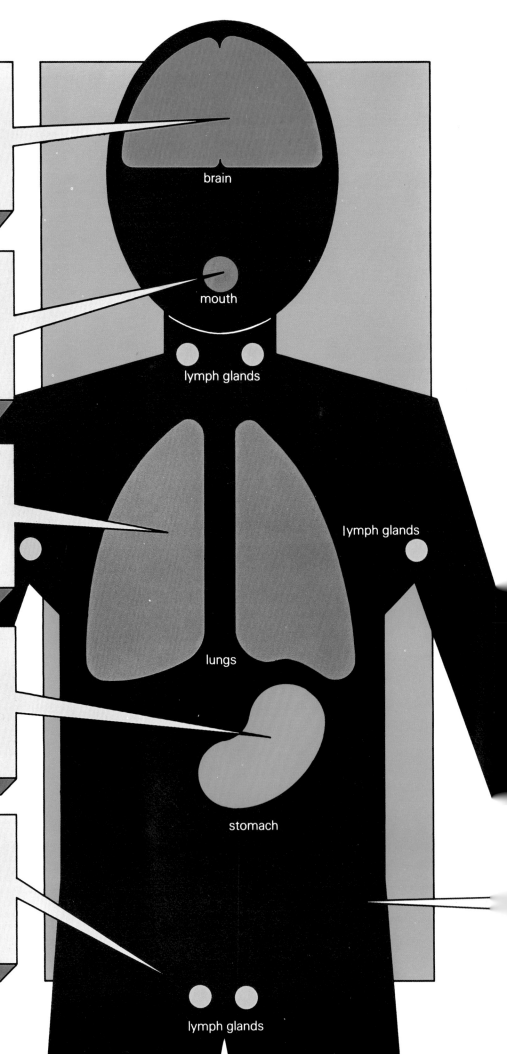

The AIDS virus can affect the brain. In adults it causes dementia (the loss of memory and control usually found among the very old), and in children it stops the brain growing.

Thrush is a thick white fungus that coats the mouth and tongue. It makes eating difficult and can spread to the esophagus, the tube down which food travels to the stomach.

Most AIDS patients develop a lung disease, PCP (*Pneumocystis carinii* pneumonia). The symptoms are fever, a dry cough and breathlessness.

Persistent diarrhea lasting for many weeks is a common symptom. This is not just a brief attack but a long-term condition, that prevents the patient digesting food properly.

Painless, hard lumps form in the glands in the neck, under the arms or in the groin. They are often one of the first signs of AIDS, but swollen glands can also be caused by many conditions.

brain

mouth

lymph glands

lymph glands

lungs

stomach

lymph glands

AIDS: the symptoms

Headache, fever and a loss of control over the muscles may result from infections affecting the brain tissue. These may also affect the patient's vision, sometimes severely.

AIDS sufferers often feel exhausted, finding it difficult to get out of bed. Night sweats and fevers may interrupt sleep. However, anxiety about AIDS can also produce these symptoms.

AIDS causes a rapid loss of weight, often 4.5kg (10lb) or more, in less than two months. As the condition worsens, the patient loses more weight until he or she is extremely weakened.

"Cold sores" caused by the herpes zoster virus are common. They are small blister-like sores found on the back, neck and face. They are very painful and persistent unless treated.

Blotches on the skin, usually purplish in color, are symptoms of Kaposi's sarcoma, a tumor which affects some AIDS victims. They look very unpleasant but are not painful.

Not everybody who carries the AIDS virus suffers from full-blown AIDS. Many carry the virus for months or years without developing the full range of symptoms – and may never do so, although it is still too early to be sure. AIDS is a "syndrome," which means that it is a pattern of diseases with different symptoms.

Some carriers develop a condition in which the lymph glands in the neck, armpits and groin are constantly swollen. They often feel tired but are otherwise normal. Others develop a condition known as AIDS-Related Complex (ARC), with symptoms including severe exhaustion, diarrhea, loss of weight, fevers and thrush – a fungal infection of the mouth.

About 15-20 per cent of these two groups of carriers go on to suffer the full range of AIDS symptoms after three years. The commonest secondary infection is an unusual form of pneumonia, found in more than half of all AIDS patients. Increasing shortness of breath, persistent dry cough and fevers are all signs of this infection, known as *Pneumocystis carinii* pneumonia (PCP). This condition can often be treated successfully if it is recognized in its very early stages.

Many AIDS patients develop a tumor called Kaposi's sarcoma, usually seen as pink or purple blotches on the skin, but also able to affect internal organs. This condition is more common among homosexuals than other AIDS patients, for reasons which are not yet clear. Some AIDS patients also suffer brain damage, known as AIDS dementia. The symptoms are loss of memory, speech difficulties and loss of control of parts of the body. Unlike the other diseases associated with AIDS, AIDS dementia is actually caused by the HIV virus.

Testing for AIDS

Scientists estimate that as many as a million and a half people in the United States carry the AIDS virus. Worldwide, the figure is a staggering ten million. Tests exist which can show whether an individual has antibodies to the HIV virus in the blood. Anyone with these antibodies probably carries the virus and is infectious. For this reason some people have recommended that everybody should be tested. But is it really a good idea?

Most doctors think not. One reason is that the tests are not 100 per cent reliable. Also it can take up to three months after a person has been in contact with the virus for the antibodies in the virus to be detectable in the blood.

▽ Blood samples are analyzed to see if they contain antibodies to the HIV virus. Antibodies in the blood indicate that the person has been infected with the virus and may be a carrier. It does not mean that the individual is suffering from AIDS, because of the virus's abilty to remain dormant for long periods. Testing too early is one reason for a false negative result, giving the all-clear to someone who is in fact a carrier.

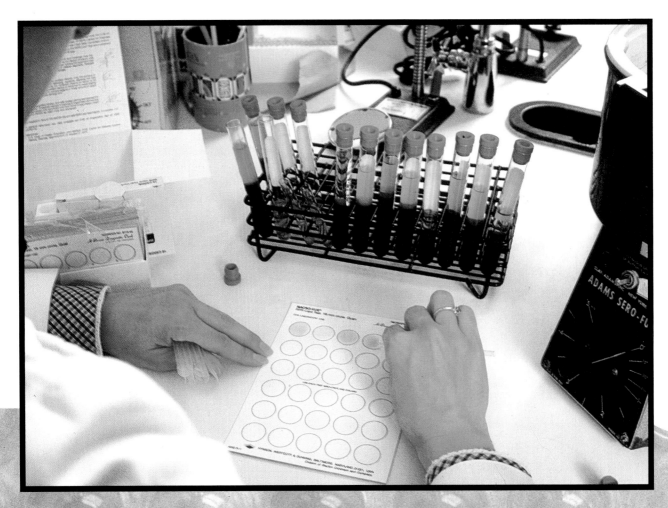

Those who were found to be antibody positive would face considerable difficulties and would gain little benefit, since there is no treatment available to rid them of the virus. They would find it difficult to get life insurance, to borrow money and to get jobs – even though they might be showing no symptoms and may never do so.

But the main danger of testing is that it can give a false security and cannot be relied upon to change people's behavior. One act of unprotected sexual intercourse with an infected partner may be enough to pass on the virus. Testing cannot be a substitute for changes in behavior. Compulsory testing for all at present offers few benefits and many risks.

▽ Counseling by a doctor, or an expert who understands the problems, can be a great help. Some specially trained counselors are now available to give advice about the HIV test and to those who are found to be carrying the virus. Below, an American doctor gives advice to a man who has just been told he is HIV positive.

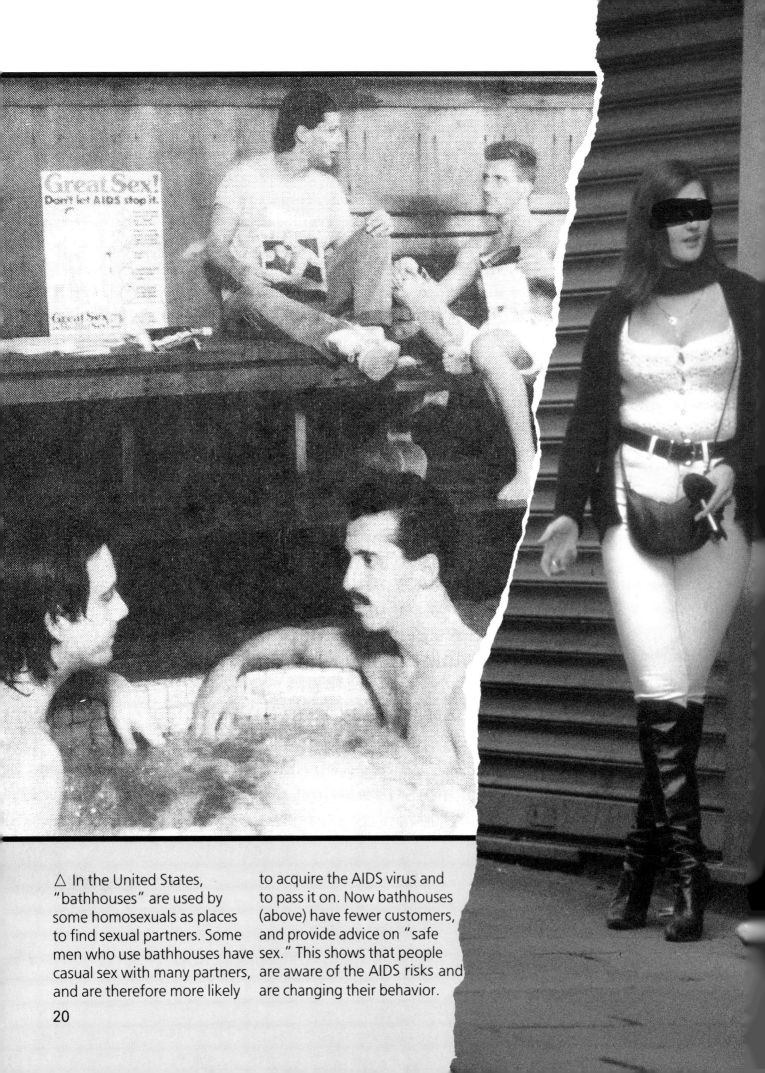

△ In the United States, "bathhouses" are used by some homosexuals as places to find sexual partners. Some men who use bathhouses have casual sex with many partners, and are therefore more likely to acquire the AIDS virus and to pass it on. Now bathhouses (above) have fewer customers, and provide advice on "safe sex." This shows that people are aware of the AIDS risks and are changing their behavior.

Avoiding AIDS

AIDS is terrifying, but like other sexually transmitted diseases, it can be avoided by taking precautions. In spite of all the scare stories, it is not caught through ordinary social contact.

Casual or promiscuous sex, especially between homosexuals, is very risky because the virus is widespread within this group. Only those in a relationship with a single sexual partner who is not already infected run no risk. Obviously this is true of both homosexual and heterosexual relationships.

But simple precautions can help reduce the risk. The easiest and most obvious is the use of a condom (a rubber sheath which is pulled over the man's penis so that semen does not enter his partner's body): that is the single most sensible thing people can do who are in any way at risk from AIDS. Anyone who is at risk from AIDS should use a condom – and not rely on the results of an AIDS antibody test. Using a condom has nothing to do with trusting a sexual partner or not. Most people who are doing the infecting do not have any symptoms. It is a matter of protection which will save lives.

For drug addicts, the best way of avoiding AIDS through infected blood is to give up injecting drugs. But if this is not possible, users need to be scrupulously careful to avoid sharing needles with other addicts.

◁ Prostitutes are at risk from the AIDS epidemic. A study of 134 prostitutes from the Rue St Denis area of Paris showed that five were carrying the AIDS virus. "Believe me, if I was a man I wouldn't come here any more," one female prostitute told the French newspaper *France-Soir*. Many prostitutes who carry the virus continue to work and therefore pass on the virus to their customers.

Preventing AIDS

Alarmed at the rapid spread of AIDS, governments around the world have begun to respond with major public health campaigns. The British Government is spending $35 million on a campaign including posters, newspaper and magazine advertising, and a leaflet to every household in the country. The campaign aims to explain the facts about AIDS, and to urge safer sexual activities, including the use of condoms, to slow down its spread.

The government also intends to provide free syringes for drug addicts. Some argue that free condoms should be given to high-risk groups.

The United States lags far behind European countries, but in 1987 TV spots began to appear. These featured the US Surgeon General, C. Everett Koop, who advocated the use of condoms.

△ Is the message getting through? Two British posters warning against the dangers of AIDS. Knowing about AIDS is the best way to combat the spread of the infection. The posters explain everyone at risk should use a condom.

There is some evidence that behavior is changing. Sales of condoms have increased in the United States, and many are changing their attitude and behavior to casual sex. "Safer sex" is now becoming fashionable, and the number of new cases of AIDS among homosexuals has actually dropped.

Drug abuse is now seen as a key way the AIDS virus is introduced to the heterosexual population. Campaigns which warn drug users of the dangers are being stepped up. In the United States 3,000 drug addicts have AIDS, 17% of the total. The sexual partners of this group are all at high risk of contracting the virus.

▽ All over the world governments and self-help groups have launched campaigns designed to encourage safer sex. The poster on a billboard in Los Angeles (below) provides a phone number to call for free advice. Posters in French and Swedish convey the same message.

23

Can AIDS be treated

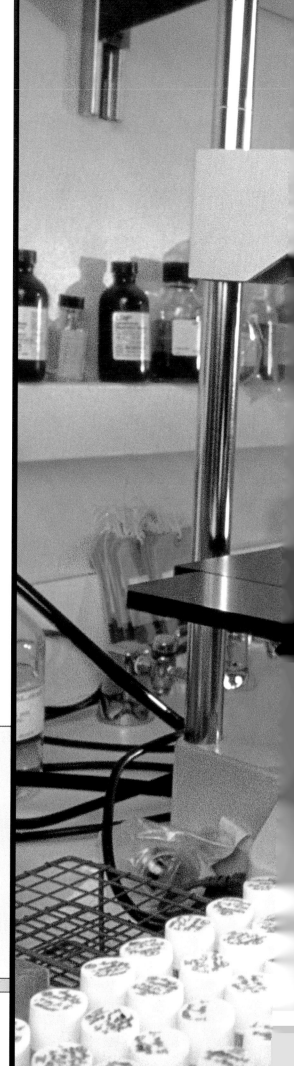

For the moment, no drugs exist to cure AIDS patients nor vaccines to prevent others catching the disease. AIDS has so far killed over 16,000 people in the United States, and within five years this figure is expected to rise to 190,000. Faced with these figures, enormous efforts are being made to find a cure.

One route is to create a vaccine which would protect people against the virus, just as the polio vaccine protects against that disease. But the task is difficult because the AIDS virus is quite variable. A vaccine effective against one variety might be useless against another. Most scientists believe it will be at least ten years, and maybe twenty, before a vaccine is available.

Treating the condition with drugs has so far proved equally frustrating. One of the most heavily publicized, azidothymidine (AZT), works by blocking the virus's ability to reproduce itself (see the diagram below). First tests with the drug have been encouraging despite the considerable problems of its side-effects. But it is not expected to be a miracle cure – it can only control the spread of the virus within the body.

▷ AZT was discovered by scientists in the laboratories of the drug company Burroughs Wellcome (right), and tested on 145 patients infected with AIDS. Another 137 patients were given a placebo (a harmless but ineffective substitute). Of the two groups, those on AZT showed signs of improving health, while those on the placebo got worse. In six months, 16 of those on the placebo died; only one of those on AZT did. Faced with these results, the American medical authorities stopped the trial in September 1986 and ordered both groups to be given AZT.

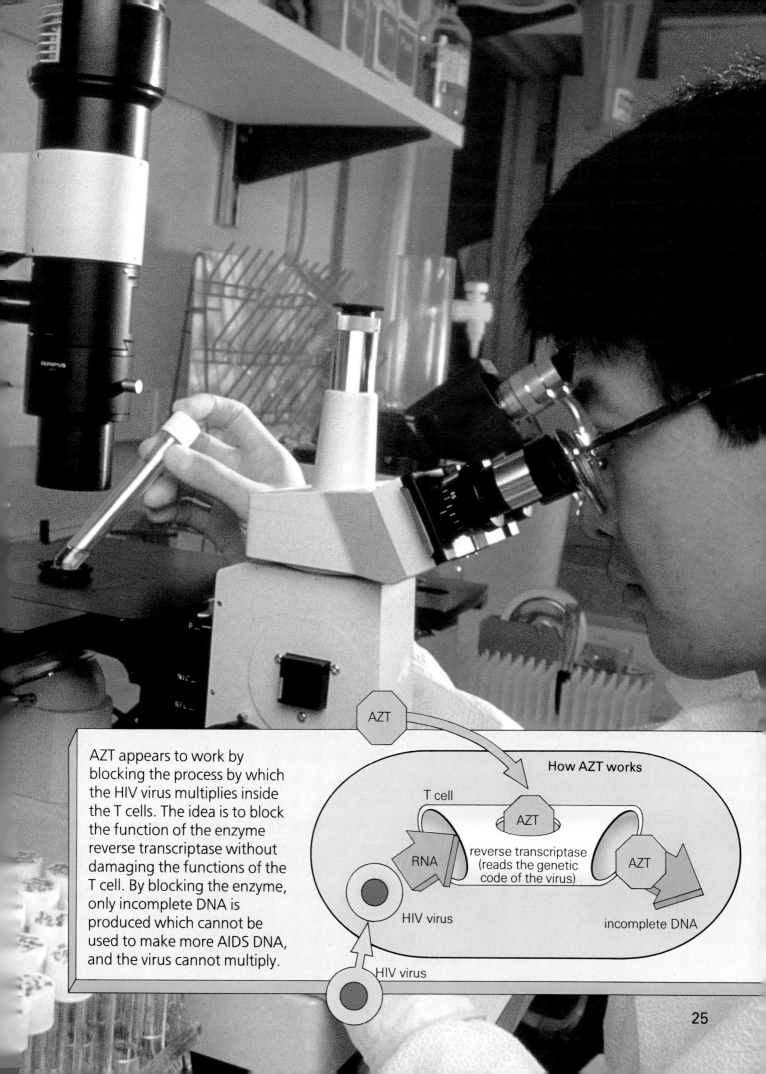

AZT appears to work by blocking the process by which the HIV virus multiplies inside the T cells. The idea is to block the function of the enzyme reverse transcriptase without damaging the functions of the T cell. By blocking the enzyme, only incomplete DNA is produced which cannot be used to make more AIDS DNA, and the virus cannot multiply.

How AZT works

T cell

AZT

reverse transcriptase
(reads the genetic
code of the virus)

RNA

AZT

incomplete DNA

HIV virus

HIV virus

25

Living with AIDS

Living with AIDS is like living with a death sentence. Some face it very calmly, others with bitter regret that they should have been selected by fate. The terrible physical effects of the condition, the exhaustion and the wasted limbs make it hard to die a dignified death. A few of those diagnosed as AIDS patients try to commit suicide, sometimes successfully, to spare themselves and their families the trauma of the long decline.

Those who do not have the full AIDS symptoms but know they are harboring the virus also face frightening pressures. Some feel they live on borrowed time, and every ache and pain brings fear that it may be the onset of the disease.

Many AIDS patients complain that nobody dares to touch them, or to kiss them, once their condition is diagnosed. One child in an American hospital had a "Do Not Touch" sign on her bed and was isolated from her parents just when she needed them most. AIDS patients need understanding and love to lighten their burden – not isolation.

◁ This is the face of AIDS. Most who die of AIDS were healthy, active individuals before the virus struck. Joseph (not his real name) was an American AIDS victim who died in June 1985.

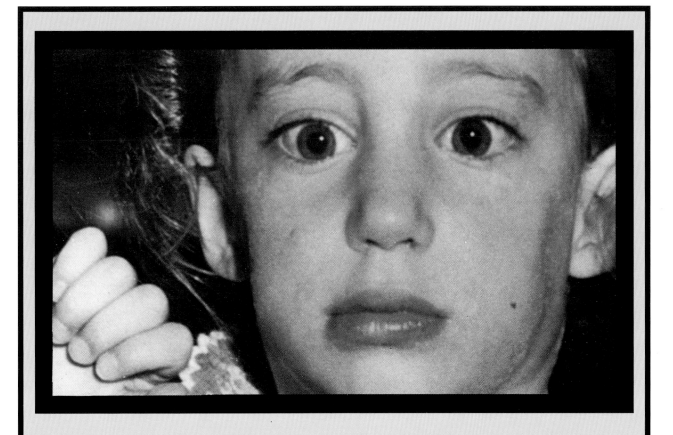

The lives of many AIDS patients are made more difficult by hostile neighbors, who fear (quite wrongly) that they or their children may be in danger of catching the disease. Some of the saddest cases involve children forced to leave schools because others refused to be taught alongside them.

Eve van Grafhorst, a four-year old sufferer, who had caught the virus through contaminated blood, had an even worse experience. Neighbors in Australia made life so difficult for Eve and her family that they were forced to leave their home and resettle elsewhere.

John (not his real name) was a patient at the Middlesex Hospital in London. He was being treated for Kaposi's sarcoma. John died in January 1987.

" A year ago all I could think about was that this disease was incurable and that I was going to die. I just wandered round the streets weeping. I was very afraid, and terrified of people knowing. I came into hospital and lay there waiting for this capsule that was going to save me. And then I realized that it didn't exist, and the only way I could tackle this illness was from within.

These months have been a struggle, and I've struggled. I care less, now, about being cured. I feel !'ve been given one more chance to deal with myself, which I should have done long ago. And I feel so much better – within myself, and about myself and my life, and this situation. "

The unknown future?

All over the world, hundreds of people die of AIDS each week. In Africa, whole families are being wiped out by the disease. Faced with such an epidemic, many countries are using massive sums of money to provide health care for those who are ill and to prepare for the future.

Many people who are ill from AIDS prefer to be looked after at home. Others prefer to go to a hospice. These are hospitals for the terminally ill that provide a calm and caring environment for those who know that their life is ending.

AIDS patients have many problems – and face a long period of knowing that they are dying. Many find it important to pass on their experience to others. Meredith Mitchell is 32 years old. She became infected with the AIDS virus from her boyfriend who was a drug addict. He has since died. She says, "The only thing I can do now is to try to help persuade the public to protect themselves and their loved ones. Remain faithful, use a condom, avoid drugs. Teach your children the real facts of life and don't discriminate against people with AIDS. They've too many problems already."

▷ An empty hospital ward, symbol of an uncertain future. The first hospital ward in the United Kingdom built for the treatment of AIDS patients has recently been opened in London. The nurse in charge is Sister Jacqui Elliot, seen here with two AIDS experts, Professor Stephen Semple (left) and Professor Michael Adler, in the ward. Much can be done to treat the infections and tumors to allow AIDS patients to lead a near-normal life for months, or even years, before they need intense hospital care.

Views on AIDS

Now that the facts are known, no one need ever catch AIDS again – if sensible precautions are taken. Here are some views of younger people about the virus and what it means to them and their future.

"AIDS can get anyone. No one knows how it started, but many people will have AIDS in the future. Women can pass it on to their babies in the womb. AIDS can kill you, but you can't catch it easily."

Ann 13

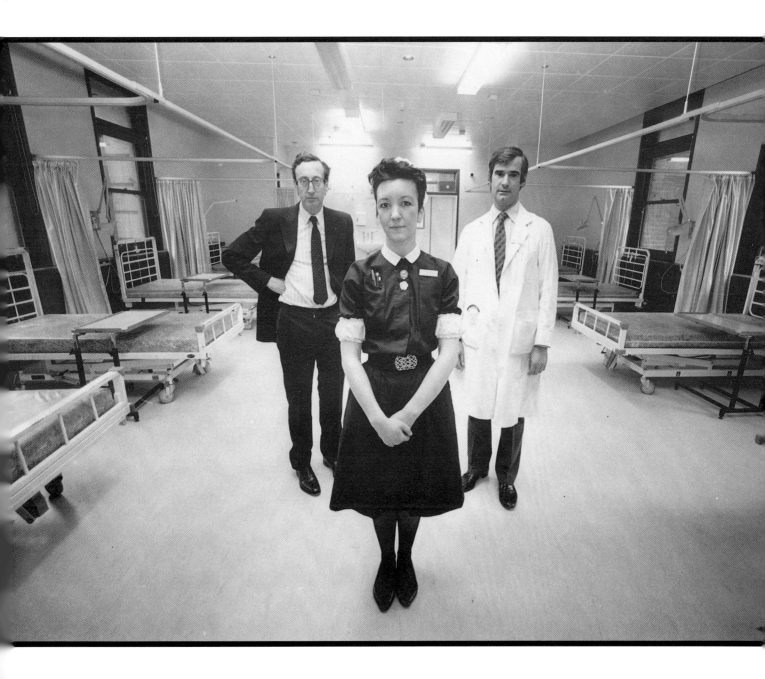

"AIDS is a dangerous disease and it can kill you and it's in the news a lot. Anyone can get it. I know because I've seen it on the posters. You can avoid it by not having sex because it's passed on in the body fluids."

Richard 13

"At first only gays could get it, but now anyone can get it. According to the ads, you must stick to one partner and wear a condom. I don't know what it will mean to me in the future."

Mark 13

Hard facts

⭐ AIDS is a worldwide epidemic of HIV infection which already affects millions of people. Most of those affected carry the AIDS virus without developing the full range of symptoms; but all those who do develop the full symptoms eventually die.

⭐ AIDS is caused by a virus, which is easy to kill outside the body. Soap and hot water are all that are needed. But once inside the bloodstream the virus is persistent and has so far defeated all efforts to find a cure.

⭐ AIDS can be avoided. It is not very easy to catch and normal social contact poses no risk. It is transmitted sexually or by the transfer of blood or blood products between people. The best hope of containing it lies in changing sexual habits, reducing the number of sexual partners and using condoms.

⭐ In the United States, by far the greatest number of AIDS victims – 66 per cent – are homosexual or bisexual men. But the virus can also be spread between men and women, and the number of women with AIDS is rising.

✪ So far, the death toll in the United States and Europe is less than 20,000 — very small when compared with earlier epidemics such as the plague (the Black Death) or the flu epidemic at the end of the First World War, which claimed 20 million victims. But nobody has really counted how many are dying in Africa, and the virus is spreading rapidly everywhere.

✪ By 1991 the United States expects to have nearly 100,000 AIDS victims: more than a hundred people will be dying of it every day. By the end of that year, the cumulative death total in the United States could be as high as 190,000.

✪ Scientists doubt that a vaccine effective against the AIDS virus can be found in less than 10 to 20 years, if ever. Until then, avoiding behavior that brings a risk of infection is the only sure way to defeat the disease. The worst catastrophes can be averted, if people at risk learn new patterns of behavior.

Index

A Africa, 4, 5, 13, 14, 28, 31
AIDS virus (HIV):
    antibody tests, 18, 19, 21
    carriers of, 6, 13, 14, 15, 17, 20, 21, 23, 30
    research into, 8-9, 10-11, 24-25, 31
    spread of, 4, 6, 7, 12, 13, 14, 15, 20, 21, 22, 23, 24, 30
antibodies, 10, 18, 19, 21
AZT (azidothymidine), 24, 25

B babies, 7, 12, 15, 28
bisexuals, 13, 31
blood, 4, 7, 12, 13, 18, 30
blood donors, 12
blood products, 7, 12, 13, 15, 30
blood transfusions, 12, 13, 15

C cases reported, 4, 5, 6, 8, 14, 23
cells, 9, 10, 11, 25
children, 4, 7, 13, 14, 15
condoms, 21, 22, 23, 28, 29, 30
counseling service, 19
cure of, 4, 24, 31

D deaths, 4, 24, 26, 27, 28, 31
doctors, 13, 19, 28
drug addicts, 8, 12, 13, 21, 22, 23, 28

E Europe, 5, 13, 14, 31

F France, 5

G Gallo, Dr. Robert, 8, 9
government campaigns, 22, 23

H hemophiliacs, 7, 8, 12, 13
heterosexuals, 7, 15, 17, 21, 23
HIV (Human Immuno-deficiency Virus), *see* AIDS virus
homosexuals, 7, 8, 13, 20, 21, 23, 30
hospices, 28
hospitals, 28-29

I immune system, 10
infection, 4, 10, 12, 13, 18, 21, 22, 23, 31

L Latin America, 5

M men, 4, 5, 13
Montagnier, Dr. Luc, 8, 9

N nurses, 13, 28

P patients, 6, 16, 17, 26, 27, 28
precautions, 4, 6, 21, 22, 23, 28, 30
prostitutes, 14, 21
public health campaigns, 22, 23

R research, 4, 8-9, 10-11, 24-25, 31

S "safe sex," 20, 22, 23
sexual behavior, 13, 19, 20, 21, 22, 23, 28, 31
sexual contact, 4, 7, 13, 15, 19, 21, 30
symptoms, 4, 6, 14, 17, 19, 21, 26, 30

T tests for, 4, 14, 18, 19, 21
treatment, 24, 26, 27, 28

U United Kingdom, 4, 12, 13, 18
United States, 4, 6, 8, 12, 13, 14, 18, 20, 24, 28, 30-31

V vaccines, 24, 31

W women, 4, 5, 7, 13, 15, 30

Photographic Credits:
Cover: Aladdin Books; pages 4/5, 6, 24/25 and 26: Colorific; page 7: Frank Fournier/Contact/Colorific; pages 8 and 9: Associated Press; pages 10/11, 18 and back cover: Science Photo Library; page 12: Ed Hooper/Picture Search; page 13: Mark Edwards/Panos Pictures; page 14: Rex Features; pages 18/19, 19, 20/21 and 27: Frank Spooner Pictures; pages 20 and 23: Alon Reininger/Contact/Colorific; page 22: Department of Health and Social Security; page 29: *The Independent* newspaper.

The quotation on page 28 appears with permission of *The Times* newspaper (January 1987).